J   Kowalski, Kathiann M.
973 Salvadorans in America
KOW

$28.00

SALVADORANS IN AMERICA

web enhanced at www.inamericabooks.com

KATHIANN M. KOWALSKI

Ŀ LERNER PUBLICATIONS COMPANY / MINNEAPOLIS

Current information and statistics quickly become out of date. That's why we developed **www.inamericabooks.com**, a companion website to the **In America** series. The site offers lots of additional information—downloadable photos and maps and up-to-date facts through links to additional websites. Each link has been carefully selected by researchers at Lerner Publishing Group and is regularly reviewed and updated. However, Lerner Publishing Group is not responsible for the accuracy or suitability of material on websites that are not maintained directly by us. It is recommended that students using the Internet be supervised by a parent, a librarian, a teacher, or another adult.

This book is dedicated to my daughter, Laura Kathryn Meissner.

Copyright © 2006 by Kathiann M. Kowalski

Lerner Publications Company
A division of Lerner Publishing Group
241 First Avenue North
Minneapolis, MN 55401 U.S.A.

Website address: www.lernerbooks.com

Library of Congress Cataloging-in-Publication Data

Kowalski, Kathiann M., 1955–
    Salvadorans in America / by Kathiann M. Kowalski.
      p.   cm. — (In America)
    Includes bibliographical references and index.
    ISBN-13: 978-0-8225-2424-3 (lib. bdg. : alk. paper)
    ISBN-10: 0-8225-2424-4 (lib. bdg. : alk. paper)
    1. Salvadoran Americans–History–Juvenile literature. 2. Salvadoran Americans–Juvenile
literature. 3. Immigrants–United States–Juvenile literature. I. Title. II. Series: In America
(Minneapolis, Minn.)
E184.S15K69 2006
973'.04687284—dc22   2004011631

Manufactured in the United States of America
1 2 3 4 5 6 – JR – 11 10 09 08 07 06

CONTENTS

INTRODUCTION

In America, a walk down a city street can seem like a walk through many lands. Grocery stores sell international foods. Shops offer products from around the world. People strolling past may speak foreign languages. This unique blend of cultures is the result of America's history as a nation of immigrants.

Native peoples have lived in North America for centuries. The next settlers were the Vikings. In about A.D. 1000, they sailed from Scandinavia to lands that would become Canada, Greenland, and Iceland. In 1492 the Italian navigator Christopher Columbus landed in the Americas, and more European explorers arrived during the 1500s. In the 1600s, British settlers formed colonies that, after the Revolutionary War (1775–1783), would become the United States. And in the mid-1800s, a great wave of immigration brought millions of new arrivals to the young country.

Immigrants have many different reasons for leaving home. They may leave to escape poverty, war, or harsh governments. They may want better living conditions for themselves and their children. Throughout its history, America has been known as a nation that offers many opportunities. For this reason, many immigrants come to America.

Moving to a new country is not easy. It can mean making a long, difficult journey. It means leaving home and starting over in an unfamiliar place. But it also means using skill, talent, and determination to build a new life. The In America series tells the story of immigration to the United States and the search for fresh beginnings in a new country—in America.

SALVADORANS IN AMERICA

Salvadorans first came to the United States more than one hundred years ago. But their numbers were very small. Large numbers of people did not come until the 1980s. At that time, El Salvador was going through a bloody civil war. People still come to the United States from El Salvador.

The census bureau says the United States was home to 765,000 people from El Salvador in 2000. But that number leaves out many people without legal papers, as well as people who were born to Salvadoran parents already living in the United States. The real total is probably closer to 1.5 million, and some sources estimate that nearly 2 million people in the United States may come from a Salvadoran background.

Salvadorans face many challenges in the United States. Many newcomers are poor. Often they speak little English. They must adjust to a new culture. Family members may be far away. Legal issues can present problems too.

Many people work long hours at low-paying jobs. Some are maids, caregivers, or gardeners. Others work at restaurants, factories, or construction sites.

Some Salvadorans in America are athletes, authors, businesspeople, and community leaders. Others are doctors or lawyers. Still more people are scholars and teachers.

Whether they are poor, rich, or in the middle class, Salvadorans in America have built new lives here. Their spirit, talents, and hard work enrich life in the United States.

1 LAND OF PRECIOUS THINGS

The Republic of El Salvador lies in Central America, a bridge of land that connects North and South America. El Salvador's 6.7 million people share a long history. That history built the country's rich cultural traditions. But it has also led to poverty, injustice, and war.

This small country measures 8,124 square miles in area—roughly the size of the state of Massachusetts. The Pacific Ocean forms the country's southern border. Guatemala is to the northwest, and Honduras lies to the northeast. Across the Gulf of Fonseca lies Nicaragua, El Salvador's eastern neighbor.

El Salvador is rich in natural beauty. The weather is warm year-round, with a wet, rainy summer and a drier winter. Thousands of plants and animals live in this tropical land. Mountains run through the country in ranges forming lines from west to east. But this dramatic landscape can be dangerous too. More than twenty of its mountain peaks are active volcanoes. Earthquakes and hurricanes often strike El Salvador as well.

AN ANCIENT LAND

People have lived in El Salvador for thousands of years. Early people lived by hunting and farming. Around A.D. 300, the area became part of the Mayan Empire. The Pokomans became the main Mayan tribe in the area. The Maya had a rich and advanced culture. Although they did not use metal tools, they built large limestone pyramids and carved huge stone statues. They also developed a writing system, and they knew a lot about astronomy and mathematics.

FIND LINKS TO LEARN MORE ABOUT THE MAYAN EMPIRE AT WWW.INAMERICABOOKS.COM.

Mayan farmers grew corn, melons, beans, and other vegetables. Cacao beans were an important and very valuable crop. People used the beans as money. Wealthy people also brewed hot chocolate with ground beans.

Later, the Pipil and Lenca tribes settled in El Salvador. By the 1000s, the Pipils were the largest and most powerful group. They spoke the language Náhuatl, and they called their homeland Cuscatlán. It means "the land of precious things."

A few Pipils were nobles, warriors, priests, or merchants. Others were potters, weavers, carpenters, or other skilled workers. But most people were farmers. Corn and cacao were still important crops. Farmers also grew cotton, bamboo, and hemp.

A Jewel of a Find

Around A.D. 600, the Laguna Caldera volcano near San Salvador—El Salvador's capital—erupted. Tons of ash and lava shot into the air, burying a nearby village in up to twenty feet of fallout. Over time, people forgot about the village. But the volcano's ash preserved many clues about its people.

In 1976 a bulldozer was digging at a construction site. It uncovered part of a Mayan farmhouse from under the ancient ash. Archaeologists came to the site. They call the site Joya de Cerén. That means "Jewel of Cerén."

Joya de Cerén in El Salvador is often called the Pompeii of the Americas. The site is unique because it is the only Mayan settlement discovered thus far (all other Mayan ruins discovered have been ceremonial sites). Above is structure 12, one of the many Mayan houses preserved at Joya de Cerén.

For archaeologists, the site really is a jewel. Archaeologists have found a dozen Mayan homes and many tools and pots. Some pots even have bits of food left in them. These things tell a lot about the ancient Maya and their daily lives.

Other places also offer a look at life long ago. Tazumál, west of the Salvadoran city of Santa Ana, showcases two flattop pyramids and stone carvings. In a courtyard, athletes probably played an ancient Mayan ball game. People may have danced on a patio.

San Andres, El Salvador, has pyramids too. They were important in Mayan religion and were built in many places throughout Central America. Other ancient sites in El Salvador are at Pampe, El Trapiche, Casa Blanca, Las Victorias, and near Lake Guija. The country's oldest archaeological sites of all are thought to be

The ruins at Tazumál are considered the most important and best-preserved in El Salvador.

caves near Corinto. Prehistoric drawings on the cave walls here may be up to ten thousand years old.

The Pipil culture was very successful. They grew enough food for their people. They had skilled craftspeople and strong armies. But in 1492, outsiders arrived in the Americas. That year the Italian explorer Christopher Columbus landed on the island of San Salvador, in the Caribbean Sea. Columbus claimed some of the land he found for Spain, which had sent him on his journey. Soon Spanish soldiers, called conquistadors, took over large parts of North and South America. They hoped to find gold and riches in this land they called the New World.

THE SPANISH CONQUEST

The Spanish army had many advantages over the local people, whom they called Indians. The

Christopher Columbus's landing on San Salvador in 1492 paved the way for other Europeans to explore the New World. The Spanish conquistadors who followed Columbus to El Salvador treated the Pipils harshly.

conquistadors had guns, while the Pipils had only spears. The Spanish brought horses to the New World and could move quickly from place to place.

The Spanish also brought disease. The Pipils and other tribes had never been exposed to European illnesses. Sickness killed thousands of people.

Spain soon conquered nearby Mexico and Guatemala. Next, it looked toward Cuscatlán. Pedro de Alvarado tried to conquer the Pipils in 1524, but they fought back fiercely. The Spanish were defeated, Alvarado was wounded, and the Pipils escaped into the mountains.

The Spanish returned to Cuscatlán the next year. In this battle and another in 1528, they conquered the region and made it one of their colonies. They founded the city of San Salvador, which means "Holy Savior," and named the area El Salvador. Spanish became the official language.

For the next three hundred years, the Spanish ruled Central America, and the Pipils' lives and culture changed dramatically. The Spanish were members of the Catholic Church, a branch of Christianity. They sent church workers called missionaries to convince the Pipils to become Catholics, and many people did become members of the Catholic Church over time. Sometimes persuasion got them to join. Other times, the Spanish used force.

Meanwhile, the ethnic makeup of the population changed as Pipils began marrying Spanish people. The children of these marriages were called mestizos. They

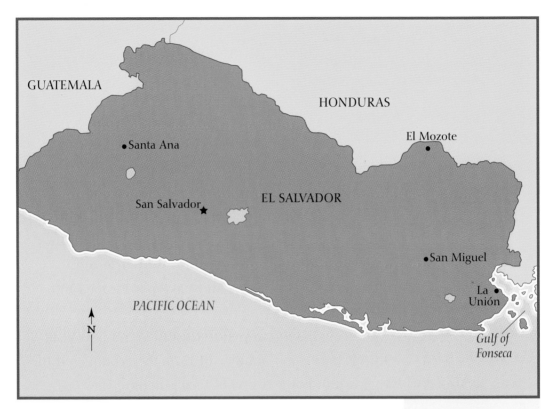

Though it is the smallest Central American country, El Salvador is the region's third most populated country. Download this and other maps at www.inamericabooks.com.

had a mixed Indian and European background. Soon only a minority of people had Pipil heritage.

The Spanish were disappointed to find that El Salvador had few precious metals or gems. But it did have fertile land. Spanish rulers began giving a few people large areas of land. The biggest landowners became known as the "Fourteen Families." While there were actually more than fourteen, the families still made up a small part of El Salvador's population. However, they held most of the nation's wealth.

THEIR CRUELTY DID NOT TAKE PITY EVEN ON WOMEN WITH CHILDREN. . . .

—*Friar Bartolemé de las Casas, criticizing the Spanish army's treatment of Central Americans during the Spanish conquest of the 1500s*

The Pipils who had been living on the land now had to work on the farms for the Spanish owners. They did backbreaking work for little money. They tended large crops of cacao. In the 1700s, demand grew for indigo—a plant used to make blue dye. Indigo turned out to be an even more valuable crop than cacao, and farm owners grew very rich.

But Spain forced El Salvador and its other colonies in the Americas to pay high taxes. It also forbade sales of cacao beans or indigo dye to anyone besides Spain. By the early 1800s, the Spanish colonies wanted change.

THE CRY FOR INDEPENDENCE

When priest José Matías Delgado rang the bells of La Merced Church on November 5, 1811, he was not calling people to worship. Rather, he and his nephew Manuel José Arce were calling upon San Salvador's people to revolt against the Spanish. The Spanish defeated that uprising and another one in 1814. But Spain could not squash

The will of the people, so decided and manifested in so many ways, cannot be called a whim, because that is never the will of a people, much less when all their wishes are directed toward being free.

—*José Matías Delgado, leader in El Salvador's struggle for independence from Spain*

CHECK OUT LINKS AT WWW.INAMERICABOOKS.COM FOR MORE INFORMATION ABOUT THE INDEPENDENCE MOVEMENT IN EL SALVADOR.

the dream of freedom. Talk of independence spread.

On September 15, 1821, Spain finally granted independence to its Central American colonies. San Salvador joined Costa Rica, Honduras, Nicaragua, and Guatemala to form a country called the United Provinces of Central America. Manuel José Arce became the new country's first president in 1825.

Too many problems plagued the new country, and by 1839 its government fell apart. The Republic of El Salvador began as an independent country in 1841.

Francisco Malespín was El Salvador's first president. For the next few decades, control went back and forth between the two main political parties, the Liberals and the Conservatives. But all the while, most of the nation's wealth still stayed within the Fourteen Families. Those families paid for the military. And the military, in turn, had strong control over the government.

By the 1850s, most of the ruling families started large farms to grow coffee. The crop offered huge profits. Soon coffee became El Salvador's major export. To make more money, El Salvador's leaders decided the country should grow even more coffee.

Until then, many rural people had been peasants, or farmers, called campesinos. Most campesinos

A peasant woman grinds corn for tortillas. El Salvador's peasants worked hard to make ends meet after the Spanish conquest.

supported their families by growing their own food on small plots of land. To let the coffee farms expand, El Salvador's leaders passed new laws that took away most of the peasants' tiny landholdings. The wealthy landowners' coffee plantations got even bigger.

Many campesinos got jobs on the big coffee plantations. They did backbreaking work to grow coffee, but they made very little money. And because they no longer had anywhere to grow their own crops, they had to buy their food. Often the wages they earned were not enough to live well. But the landless peasants had little choice but to keep working on the plantations.

SALVADORANS ARRIVE IN THE UNITED STATES

The coffee trade grew, and the United States became the biggest market for El Salvador's coffee. Wealthy farm owners in El Salvador wanted to keep their

Many Salvadoran campesinos worked as coffee pickers. This young woman holds a basket full of coffee berries she has just picked.

15

American customers happy, so they formed ties with merchants and people who ran shipping companies. The ties helped the companies in the United States too.

As a result of these ties, a few well-to-do Salvadorans moved to the United States. Mainly, they went to San Francisco, California, a major shipping port. Other Salvadorans got jobs with the shipping companies, and some of them settled in the United States too.

Later on, the United States built the Panama Canal across a narrow strip of land in the Central American country of Panama. The canal's purpose was to make travel between the Atlantic and Pacific oceans easier and faster, and it was a huge construction job. Some peasants looking for jobs left El Salvador and went south. They joined the throngs working on the canal.

After the canal was finished, new shipping routes opened up between Central America and U.S. cities. Many Salvadorans who had worked on building the canal got jobs with the shipping lines. Over time, some of them moved to the United States. Usually, they settled in cities where the shipping companies had offices.

LA MATANZA: THE SLAUGHTER

Back in El Salvador, the peasants' situation stayed bleak. Then, in 1929, the Great Depression began. The depression was a serious economic downturn in the United States and other countries. Nations that had been big buyers of Central American coffee suddenly couldn't pay as much for coffee as they had before. As coffee prices dropped, so did coffee farmers' wages. Many people were starving. Once again, the nation needed change.

In 1932 the common people's unrest exploded in a revolt led by Augustin Farabundo Martí.

Farabundo Martí came from one of the landowning families, but he read books by Karl Marx and other writers about Communism. Moved by their ideas, he eventually became the leader of El Salvador's Communist Party.

WHAT IS COMMUNISM?

Augustin Farabundo Martí was the head of El Salvador's Communist Party. Communism is a political and economic system based on the idea of shared property. In a Communist nation, the government controls all land and other resources in the name of the people. In theory, the government can then give out benefits fairly, based on people's needs.

In practice, however, Communist countries have not been able to meet all their people's basic needs. Beyond that, Communist nations have often exercised strong control over many areas of everyday life. In many cases, they have limited what individual people are allowed to do.

Communism was a very unpopular idea in some places, including the United States. Many Americans felt that the system went against democracy and freedom. They feared such wide-sweeping government control.

But the Communist Party found followers in El Salvador. The poor there were tired of some people having so much, while others had so little. To them, starving and living in poverty were not freedom. They felt anything had to be better than what they had.

And he convinced others that revolt against the government was the only way to change things in El Salvador. Many peasants joined in the revolt, including many Pipils.

El Salvador's president, Maximiliano Hernández Martínez, reacted quickly and forcefully. His army crushed the revolt, and his soldiers killed Farabundo Martí and the people who had helped him. Because many Pipils had been part of the revolt, the soldiers also killed anyone they could find who was Pipil—even if they had not done anything wrong. About thirty thousand people died in two months. The massacre became known as La Matanza, or the slaughter.

After La Matanza, many Pipils were afraid to practice their traditions openly. They would not even speak their own language in public. As time went on, the ancient Pipil culture slowly disappeared until very little was left of that group's traditions. Meanwhile, the failed revolution left many things unchanged. Military rule continued into the 1940s and 1950s. A few families still held most of the wealth, and the peasants stayed very poor.

IT CONVERTED THE CAPITAL INTO A CEMETERY. . . . NO ONE WENT OUT BECAUSE OF FEAR.

—*Joaquín Castro Canizales, remembering La Matanza*

MORE MOVES

Throughout this time, small numbers of Salvadorans continued to come to the United States. Some of them were well off. They came to visit and then stayed. Or they came north because of business or diplomatic (government) programs.

Some Salvadoran peasants went north to Mexico and joined the Bracero Program there. Starting in 1942, that program brought workers north to do farmwork in the United States. Most braceros, or hired hands, later went back to Mexico. Yet many stayed in Southern California. They made new homes there.

Other people got jobs in American factories. During the 1940s, the United States was in World War II (1939–1945). The Korean War followed in the early 1950s, and during the 1960s, the United States became involved in the Vietnam War (1956–1975). Also, for more than forty years, the United States and the Soviet Union were involved in the Cold War (1945–1991). In this long, tense conflict, the two countries did not actually fight a war. However, the

Migrant workers in the Bracero Program harvest crops on a California farm. The Bracero Program provided California farms with thousands of laborers from Central America.

United States wanted to be ready just in case. It wanted ships, planes, bombs, and other equipment. All of this activity created jobs, and some Salvadorans worked for companies linked to wartime industries.

Ties between America and El Salvador increased during the 1960s. To take advantage of lower costs, American companies built factories in El Salvador. They made cloth, paper, and other products. As a result, El Salvador became the most industrialized country in Central America. Peasants from the countryside flooded into the cities to work. But factory wages were very low.

Nevertheless, contact with the American companies that ran the factories helped create more connections between El Salvador and the United States. More people came north to America. In large

Salvadoran women work in a **maquila,** *a U.S.-owned clothing factory in El Salvador. Cheap labor was one of the advantages for U.S. businesses in El Salvador.*

part, where people went determined what type of jobs they could get. Some Salvadorans went to Los Angeles, California, where they often got jobs in the garment industry, making clothes. Salvadorans who went to Long Island, New York, often became housekeepers and gardeners.

Diplomatic contacts (links to people in government and political agencies) also brought workers north. In many cases, Americans from Washington, D.C., worked for a while in El Salvador. Later, when they came back to the United States, they might bring their Salvadoran housekeepers too. Those immigrants later brought other family members to the United States.

The United States was still home to very few Salvadorans compared to other immigrant groups. Often Salvadoran immigrants had to work at jobs that did not pay a lot. Many of them suffered discrimination too. But Salvadorans made new homes in the United States. They paved the way for waves of Salvadoran immigrants who would come later.

2 FLEEING FROM WAR

Throughout the 1970s, El Salvador's major landowners stayed wealthy. But the plight of the peasants grew worse. The country's huge growth in population was one problem. In 1950 El Salvador had 1.9 million people. By 1975 the country had 4.1 million people.

While the number of people more than doubled, the land and resources did not. Many peasants went to Honduras, but war broke out between the two countries in 1969. About 200,000 people had to go back to El Salvador. The country had little enough for its peasants before. Now there was even less.

Many peasants became migrant workers—laborers who move from place to place following seasonal jobs. In many cases, migrant workers traveled without their families. If the families came along, they would all crowd into a single room, usually near a big farm. They often had to cook outside and share a single bathroom and showers with other workers and their families.

Other rural Salvadorans flocked to El Salvador's cities, but jobs were hard to find and paid very little. Some families shared tiny apartments. Many others lived in shacks made of metal and scrap lumber. Often they did not even have access to clean drinking water or basic sewer systems. These conditions led to many health problems.

In addition, many families could not afford to send their children to school, so many young people could not read. That made it even more unlikely that peasants could ever change their lives.

Many of the job seekers who came to El Salvador's cities could not afford apartments. They crowded into slums and shantytowns, such as the one below, on the edge of San Salvador.

Meanwhile, the Salvadoran army still held a lot of power. Its leaders wanted to protect the status quo. That is, they liked things just the way they were and wanted to keep them that way. Many Salvadorans felt hopeless. The present system was not doing anything to help poor people.

But some groups talked about change. To them, a Communist system in which everyone shared wealth seemed like it would be fairer. To change society in El Salvador, these groups wanted to redistribute wealth. Workers and peasants would get more, while rich people would give some up. If rich people would not agree to that, the leaders felt, the peasants should take charge. They could rebel against the existing government.

Several of these groups joined together. They became the Farabundo Martí National Liberation Front, or FMLN for short. Farabundo Martí had led the failed peasants'

Young members of the FMLN gather in the Salvadoran countryside.

revolt in 1932. Although the government had put him to death, people remembered Farabundo Martí as a force for change.

El Salvador's wealthy people felt threatened by these groups. They did not want to give up their property. They still controlled the army, and they wanted the army's leaders to crush any rebel activity.

Death squads organized by the army set out to kill anyone

Before I left. . . , I lost my first brother, who was assassinated together with several other friends, including a cousin of mine. They were brutally killed by the death squads. . . . And later on they killed two other brothers.

—Carlos Vaquerano, executive director, Salvadoran American Leadership and Educational Fund (SALEF), who fled El Salvador at the age of 15

suspected of ties to a rebel group. The squads were groups of soldiers who committed kidnapping, torture, and murder. Victims did not get a hearing or trial, and they did not even have to be guilty of anything. The death squads did not have to account for their actions, either. They had a license to kill, and with the army's unspoken blessing, they used it.

Abuses of human rights became common, while terror grew among the people. Yet people's desire for change did not die. If anything, El Salvador's poor people wanted change more than ever.

WAR BEGINS

In 1979 a group of civilians and army leaders took over the government. This group wanted to make reforms to help the people of El Salvador. But they soon found that they could not control the army. Without that power, they could not make needed changes.

Early the next year, a new group took over. They, too, promised to make changes and stop the terror. But the violence went on. Death squads still roamed the countryside.

Meanwhile, the Catholic Church in El Salvador had begun to speak out against the death squads. For a long time, the church had backed the government. But by the end of the 1970s, some church leaders were speaking up for the peasants. They wanted people to be free from unjust treatment. In their eyes, good Christians should help the poor, even if that meant changing the social system.

Oscar Arnulfo Romero was the archbishop (a high-ranking church official) of El Salvador at this time. Like many other priests, he had supported the nation's leaders at first. But then assassins working for the government killed one of his close friends. After

I BESEECH YOU, I BEG YOU, I ORDER YOU, IN THE NAME OF GOD, TO STOP THE REPRESSION!

—*Archbishop Oscar Romero, in his last sermon, March 23, 1980*

Archbishop Oscar Romero performs Mass at a cathedral in San Salvador. He became an important critic of El Salvador's corrupt government.

that, Romero criticized El Salvador's leaders. He spoke out against violence and injustice.

Romero soon began receiving death threats. But he kept speaking out. On Sunday, March 23, 1980, Romero gave one of his most passionate sermons. He begged El Salvador's soldiers to stop killing people. No matter what their leaders told them, Romero said, killing was wrong.

The next day, Romero went to say Mass (a Catholic church service) at a hospital chapel. Without warning, an assassin shot and killed him during the service. To make matters worse, snipers also shot into the crowd at Romero's funeral Mass.

Romero's murder was a turning point for Salvadorans. The nation was already outraged by the violence. Now, it seemed, the government would stop at nothing to silence anyone who disagreed with it. If not even the leading church official was safe, people feared, then no one was. The murder of Romero, who had fought for the common people's rights, sparked civil war in El Salvador.

A NATION TORN APART

The civil war that erupted after Romero's death was long and bloody. At first, the FMLN hoped for an early victory. They fought very hard, but the army fought back.

El Salvador's government asked the United States for help. The United States had been involved in Central America for a long time. American companies had factories and property there.

Reports of violence by the Salvadoran army troubled some people in the United States. Nearby Cuba and Nicaragua—both Communist-led nations—were helping the Salvadoran rebels with money they got from the Communist Soviet Union. Leaders in the United States were afraid that if the rebels won in El Salvador, they might set up a Communist government there.

Because of these fears, the United States agreed to send economic aid to El Salvador's leaders. As the war dragged on, the total came to billions of U.S. dollars. El Salvador's army used the U.S. money to buy weapons. The money helped keep the army going so it could fight the FMLN.

But the army attacked other people too. In late 1980, for example, soldiers attacked and killed four American women working in El Salvador as missionaries. The next year, soldiers entered the village of El Mozote and killed more than two hundred men, women, and children. No one in the government did anything to stop the soldiers' violence.

After the El Mozote tragedy, the United States pressed El Salvador to make reforms. But the United States also kept sending large amounts of money. The FMLN soon saw that it could not win the war quickly, and the rebels switched their strategy. They tried to wear down the army bit by bit by launching small surprise attacks. Violence continued on both sides.

Ordinary people could not stay out of the war, even if they wanted to. In many cases, both the army and the FMLN forced people to become soldiers. They dragged young men away from their families. They made many children become soldiers.

Fear gripped the Salvadoran people. Citizens began to tell the army if they thought a neighbor or someone else they knew backed the rebels. Most people

Not even children could escape the horrors of El Salvador's civil war. Most boys twelve years old—and sometimes younger—were routinely forced to fight on one side of the conflict or the other.

FIND LINKS TO LEARN MORE ABOUT EL SALVADOR'S LONG AND BLOODY CIVIL WAR AT WWW.INAMERICABOOKS.COM.

THE ARMY CAME TO MY NEIGHBORHOOD LOOKING FOR ME. SO, I DIDN'T HAVE THE CHANCE TO THINK VERY MUCH ABOUT THE TRIP. ONE DAY I HAD TO GET AWAY FROM THE HOUSE.

—Saul Solorzano, who fled El Salvador at the age of 17

did this because they were afraid of being accused of supporting the rebels themselves. But it meant that people could not trust each other anymore.

Salvadorans had good reason to be afraid. Soldiers arrested or kidnapped thousands of innocent people. Many of them were never heard from again. Some died painful deaths. Others were finally set free after being tortured.

Still other people received death threats. The army came looking for one high school student because he took part in his church youth group. A nurse was threatened after she bandaged a wounded man who came to her door one night. College students were targeted based on the classes they took. People who got such threats often left the country if they could. Anything seemed better than sticking around for the death squads.

Meanwhile, gunfire often rang out on the streets. Schools and factories shut down. When they did stay open, people were often afraid to leave their homes. They did not want to be in the cross fire.

Even when bullets weren't flying, people suffered. Making a living had been hard enough before the war, but now it became almost impossible. For many people, leaving home began to seem like the only way to survive.

A DANGEROUS JOURNEY

The civil war forced up to one-fourth of El Salvador's people to leave their homes. Some went to different parts of the country. They hoped that their enemies would not find them. Other Salvadorans went to Guatemala or Mexico. But most went farther north to the United States.

Some Salvadorans entered the country legally. They had official government papers and could get jobs. But most Salvadorans who came had no legal papers.

Desperate to escape the violence in El Salvador, they simply fled to the United States without getting legal permission. These immigrants became known as "undocumented migrants." Sometimes they were also called "illegal aliens."

Entering the United States illegally was very dangerous. First, Salvadorans had to cross at least two countries—Guatemala and

LEAVING LOVED ONES BEHIND

Many Salvadorans who fled from the civil war could not bring their families with them. Either they had too little time to escape or they did not have enough money. Families were split apart as husbands left behind wives and children or women left children and their fathers. Young teenagers often had to flee on their own, leaving behind parents, brothers, and sisters. In some cases, families were never able to get back together again—either in El Salvador or in the United States.

Because of this, many people felt very lonely once they got to the United States. They might know a relative or acquaintance in their new country, but the people they loved most were still behind in El Salvador. That loneliness added to the feelings of pain and sadness that many immigrants already felt about leaving their homes.

Mexico. Robbers and thieves often waited along the way. Then Salvadoran immigrants still had to cross the border into the United States, which was guarded in many places.

Many Salvadorans paid coyotes, or smugglers, to help them enter the United States. Coyotes charged hundreds of dollars to sneak immigrants with no legal papers across the border. This fee was huge for most Salvadorans struggling just to get by. And once someone scraped together the money to pay a coyote, they received no guarantees. If a coyote failed, he or she often kept the money. Anyone who wanted to try again would have to come up with more money. Some coyotes even held immigrants hostage until a friend or relative paid still more money to let them go.

Coyotes find many creative ways to sneak illegal immigrants across the Mexico–United States border, but these efforts often fail. The U.S. border patrol uses advanced technology, such as X-ray equipment, to scan trucks (below) *for illegal immigrants.*

Coyotes often cared little about their clients' safety. They sometimes tried to smuggle immigrants into the United States by packing them into the trunks of cars. Some of these immigrants suffocated before they crossed the border. Other times, coyotes made people wade or swim across the Rio Grande—the river separating Mexico from Texas—and some immigrants drowned. In other cases, coyotes marched people across the desert of the southwestern United States. Many immigrants died from heat, thirst, or starvation. But most people without legal papers had no other choice than to hire a coyote and no way to stop this kind of treatment.

U.S. border guards presented yet another challenge. They arrested people who were caught trying to cross the border illegally. The government would then deport those people, or send them back to their home country. But the civil war was still raging in El Salvador, and most people who were sent back were too afraid to stay there. Many tried to cross the border multiple times before they finally made it into the United States.

A U.S. border patrol agent scans an area near the border between Eagle Pass, Texas, and Mexico for illegal immigrants. Thousands of undocumented immigrants enter the United States every year along the Mexican border. Some immigrants are allowed to stay here, but many more are sent back to their countries of origin.

FINDING NEW HOMES

Once they were in the United States, most newcomers still had a long way to go. Many people went to cities where other Salvadorans had gone before them. This common pattern is called a migration chain.

The earliest immigrants from El Salvador had gone to San Francisco. New arrivals with any connections to those people went there.

But the greatest number of people went to Los Angeles. Some Salvadorans had already moved there, and Los Angeles had jobs available. In addition, Los Angeles's warm weather and its location near the Pacific Ocean made people feel closer to El Salvador.

FOLK DANCING

El Salvador has a rich history of folk dancing *(below)*, with lively music and colorful costumes. Salvadorans brought their love of music and folk dances when they came to the United States.

"El Carbonero" is about a man who comes down the mountain to sell charcoal. Other favorite folk dances are "The Dance of the Little Bull," "The Dance of the Tiger," and "The Dance of the Wild Pig."

Salvadorans moved to areas of the United States that already had large Spanish-speaking immigrant communities with Spanish-owned businesses. Banding together with other immigrants who spoke their language helped them better adjust to their new home.

Los Angeles also has many barrios, neighborhoods where Spanish is spoken. Most barrio residents are Hispanic—people whose families come from Mexico, Central America, and South America. Another word that means the same thing is "Latino." By living in the barrios, Salvadorans did not have to struggle with English at home. They could speak Spanish in stores, at restaurants, in churches, and at community centers. And while El Salvador's culture is unique, many Salvadorans felt more at home with other Hispanic people.

MANY PEOPLE ARE INTERESTED IN LEARNING ABOUT THEIR FAMILY'S HISTORY. THIS STUDY IS CALLED GENEALOGY. IF YOU'D LIKE TO LEARN ABOUT YOUR OWN GENEALOGY AND HOW YOUR ANCESTORS CAME TO AMERICA, VISIT WWW.INAMERICABOOKS.COM FOR TIPS AND LINKS TO HELP YOU GET STARTED. THERE YOU'LL ALSO FIND TIPS ON RESEARCHING NAMES IN YOUR FAMILY HISTORY.

More and more Salvadorans came to Los Angeles. They moved to different Hispanic neighborhoods spread out over a big area. Some areas were especially popular, such as the Pico-Union area and parts of Van Nuys and Hollywood.

On the one hand, Salvadorans' new neighborhoods in Los Angeles offered low rent and a community of other Spanish speakers. But that low rent often paid for old, overcrowded housing. Crime rates were high. Still, Salvadorans kept coming to Los Angeles. Eventually, more Salvadorans lived there than in any city in the world besides San Salvador.

Many other Salvadorans went to Washington, D.C. Salvadorans who had moved there before the war helped family and friends find jobs. At that time in the 1980s, large numbers of American women began taking jobs outside the home. That change created more demand for workers to clean houses or take care of children. Salvadoran women were glad to take those jobs, even if they paid very little.

A lot of building went on around Washington in the 1980s too, creating jobs in construction. Salvadoran men could make more at those jobs than they could doing restaurant work,

Salvadoran construction workers mix plaster at their job site in California.

cleaning, or gardening. Salvadorans also liked Washington's international flavor. They did not feel quite so out of place there.

Long Island, New York, was also a major destination. About one thousand Salvadorans had lived there before the civil war. During the civil war, most of their hometowns back in El Salvador were the scene of intense fighting.

When people fled those towns, they went to where they knew someone.

"You can almost match one village in El Salvador to one village on Long Island," notes Patrick Young, the program director at the Central American Refugee Center in New York (CARECEN–NY). For example, most people from Polorós in eastern El Salvador fled to Glen Cove on Long Island.

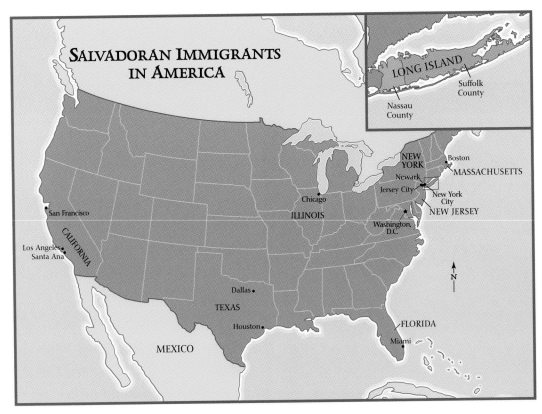

Salvadorans have formed strong communities throughout the United States.
Visit www.inamericabooks.com to download this and other maps.

Salvadorans went to areas near Long Island too. New York City is home to many Salvadorans, along with Jersey City and Newark in New Jersey. Other people went to the Texas cities of Houston and Dallas, which were growing rapidly in the 1980s. Still others settled in Chicago, Illinois; Miami, Florida; and Boston, Massachusetts. Many of these Salvadoran newcomers moved into local barrios, often living in very cramped quarters. Most were willing to take whatever low-paying jobs they could get.

Salvadorans' numbers in the United States swelled during the 1980s. In just ten years, the number jumped at least 500 percent. In a 1990 report, the census bureau said almost half a million foreign-born Salvadorans lived in the United States. But the actual figure was probably much higher. People who had come into the country illegally did not want to be found by the U.S. government, so they tried to avoid being counted by census surveys.

PROBLEMS WITHOUT PAPERS

During the 1980s, the United States took a strong stand against illegal aliens. Many U.S. citizens had started to worry about the large number of immigrants—both legal and illegal. Some thought that the newcomers were taking jobs away from them. Others did not want their taxes to pay for the social services those people might need. Still other people felt uneasy about the way the country's ethnic makeup was changing.

In response to these worries, the government began enforcing immigration laws more strictly. It passed new laws making it harder to get into the country. These laws also made it tougher for people who immigrated illegally to stay if they were found.

The new laws made life harder for Salvadorans in America who did not have the right legal papers. The war was still going on at home, and people were afraid to go back. Some Salvadorans felt so afraid that they rarely went out, for fear that the Immigration and Naturalization Service (INS) would find them.

The same fear of being deported often kept people from going to clinics, shelters, and other places set up to help poor people. Finding a good job became much harder too. Places that were willing to hire people who came into the country illegally usually paid very low

An undocumented Salvadoran immigrant awaits word of his fate at the INS detention center in San Francisco, California.

wages. In many cases, they did not follow rules about worker health and safety. But employees were afraid that if they complained, their boss might call the INS.

Many Salvadorans hid in fear, but some of them started groups to help their people. Early on, the groups held protest marches and took other steps to tell people about the terror back in El Salvador. The groups wanted the United States to stop helping the army there, and they wanted better treatment in the United States for people who fled the war.

The groups also helped people seek asylum, or government protection. By law, the INS could let people stay in the United States if their home country persecuted them or if they had a real fear of going back. With the brutal civil war still raging in El Salvador, people felt very afraid.

But the United States was still sending lots of money to El Salvador. It still saw the nation as a good place to do business. If it granted asylum, it would be saying

that the Salvadoran army persecuted people. That would not look good to the world, and U.S. taxpayers would object. To save face, the government denied most of the Salvadorans' requests.

Several churches in the United States joined Salvadoran groups' efforts to keep people from being sent away. Among other things, the churches in this Sanctuary Movement helped feed and house Salvadorans who came into the country illegally to escape war in their homeland. The churches and Central American immigrants also sued the government to get fair treatment on asylum claims.

While Salvadorans eventually won some victories, legal issues dragged on for years. Salvadoran groups kept working to change U.S. immigration laws.

CHECK OUT
WWW.INAMERICABOOKS.COM
FOR LINKS TO MORE
INFORMATION ABOUT
SALVADORANS' INVOLVEMENT
IN IMMIGRATION LAW.

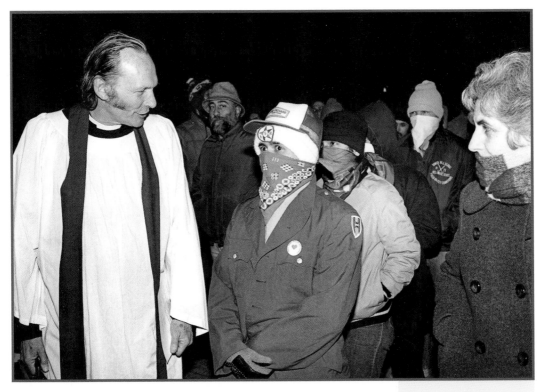

WEARY OF WAR

In December 1989, Salvadorans in the United States were shocked to hear that soldiers in El Salvador had killed six Jesuit priests at a university in San Salvador. The soldiers had also killed the priests' housekeeper and her daughter. The government denied any wrongdoing, but people were outraged. Salvadorans in the United States and human rights groups joined together and protested against America's support of the violent war.

This time, the U.S. government took another look at its relationship with El Salvador. America was getting tired of paying billions of dollars for a war that never seemed to end. And Communism's spread in Central America didn't seem as threatening

A priest from the Sanctuary Movement speaks with Salvadoran refugees (people who have fled their homelands to escape danger) in Washington, D.C.

anymore, especially after the
Soviet Union—which had
supported Communism's spread—
crumbled in 1991.

El Salvador was weary of the
war too. Finally, on January 16,
1992, the government and the
FMLN rebels signed a peace
agreement. El Salvador would cut
the number of soldiers in its army

FOR MORE INFORMATION
ABOUT EL SALVADOR'S
1992 PEACE TREATY, CHECK
WWW.INAMERICABOOKS.COM
FOR LINKS.

by half and pass laws to protect
human rights. The rebel groups
would become lawful political
parties that could take part in
democratic elections.

On January 16, 1992, FMLN leader Joaquín Villalobos signs a peace agreement known as the Chapultepec Peace Accords, officially marking the end of twelve years of civil war in El Salvador.

FINDING THE FACTS

Formed in 1945, the United Nations (UN) works to promote peace and well-being around the world. To learn the truth about El Salvador's civil war, the UN set up a group to find the facts. The group published its report in 1993. It was more than seventy-three thousand words long and went into great detail about the war's violence. In describing the 1981 El Mozote attack, the report noted, "The victims at El Mozote were left unburied. During the weeks that followed the bodies were seen by many people who passed by there." The report also discussed killings by death squads and how soldiers murdered priests, nuns, judges, and mayors.

Both sides had done awful things during the war, but the Salvadoran army was behind most of the worst cases. However, El Salvador's leaders did not punish the people named in the report. Instead, they pardoned them (did not charge them with any crimes) and said that the country should move on. Many people felt that decision was wrong.

Not everyone got away without punishment, however. In 2002 three Salvadoran torture victims who had moved to Florida sued two former army generals who had moved there too. The U.S. court ruled that the generals must pay more than $54 million to the victims. And in 2004, a court decided that another Salvadoran military commander who moved to California was partially responsible for Archbishop Oscar Romero's assassination in 1980. The court called the murder a "crime against humanity." Such rulings recognize that people in El Salvador violated basic human rights during the war.

El Salvador's civil war was over, but its scars remained. More than seventy-five thousand people had died. Many others had disappeared. It seemed that nearly every Salvadoran—both in El Salvador and in America—had lost at least one friend, family member, or neighbor. And almost everyone also knew someone who had left the country.

In 1988 I left the country [El Salvador], because the situation was not very good. I had a family, and I was tired of seeing so much violence.
I was not doing anything for my family or for myself there.

—Dina López, geology professor, Ohio State University

3

MEETING MODERN CHALLENGES

Salvadorans kept coming to the United States throughout the 1990s and into the twenty-first century. They came to join family members who had come during the war and made new homes here. Salvadorans also kept coming to escape the poverty, crime, and unrest that still troubled their homeland. People also wanted to make a new start after earthquakes and other natural disasters struck.

About one-fourth of all Salvadorans live in the United States, and they continue to arrive. Salvadorans want to build a new life in America. As a group, though, they face huge challenges.

FACING BARRIERS

Most Salvadorans do not speak English when they arrive in the United States. This language barrier presents many challenges. Without basic English skills, immigrants

Family is an important aspect of Salvadoran life.

have a hard time finding good jobs or dealing with other Americans. Children who don't speak English have a harder time in school.

Learning English is hard for anyone in a new culture. It is even harder for many Salvadorans if they have had little schooling back home. "It's difficult to learn English if you can't read and write in Spanish," notes Patrick Young at CARECEN–NY.

Other barriers are less obvious but just as real. For example, many Salvadoran Americans live in neighborhoods with other Spanish–speaking people. Ethnic neighborhoods can build a sense of community. But many people in these areas have little contact with non–Hispanics. With limited interaction and information beyond their neighborhoods, Salvadorans may feel as if they're not part of America as a whole.

Beyond these obstacles, some Salvadorans face discrimination—unfair treatment based on their ethnic background. U.S. history contains many cases of longtime Americans treating immigrant groups badly. Federal and state laws outlaw certain kinds of discrimination. But fear, resentment, or other reasons still cause some people to be biased against recent immigrants or other groups.

MAKING ENDS MEET

Many Salvadorans came to the United States with almost nothing. Often they still owed money for their trip. Once they arrived, they needed food and clothes. In many cases, friends or relatives who had immigrated earlier were too poor themselves to offer much help.

Newcomers often can't pay for good housing either. Single people often double up and share rooms in tiny apartments. Or a whole family may crowd into an apartment's one bedroom while two or three other people take the living room. Sometimes a dozen or more people cram into homes built for one family.

Finding jobs is another challenge. Poor English and limited skills make good jobs hard to get. Without legal papers, people have even fewer options. As a result, many Salvadorans take dead-end jobs with little chance to move ahead. Usually they do hard, physical work for very low wages. They rarely have health insurance or other benefits.

Many Salvadoran American women clean houses. Some are live-in maids, while others go from house to house. Other Salvadoran women become nannies or other in-home caregivers. A woman may take care of children whose parents both work. Meanwhile, her own children may be back in El Salvador. Or if they are in the United States, they may not have good day care.

A lot of Salvadorans work long hours in clothing factories. The work is tedious and frequently pays employees based on the number of items they work on. This payment can often be less than the legal minimum wage.

Many Salvadoran men work in landscaping. Other men do commercial cleaning. Restaurants also attract immigrant workers, where people become dishwashers, bus staff, and assistant cooks. Construction work pays better than some other jobs, but there are fewer jobs when the economy is slow. Also, construction work is hard and sometimes dangerous.

A Salvadoran woman washes dishes in a Washington, D.C., restaurant.

Other people do not have steady jobs. In large cities, they gather at corners or trailers. They hope

Many Salvadorans who cannot find steady work wait on corners and in parking lots for employers to offer them jobs. These men are known as day laborers.

someone will come along to offer them a day job. If they are lucky, they might make fifty dollars working very long hours. But often they go home with nothing, only to come back the next day.

Even many educated Salvadorans may face limited choices. Many times they don't know anyone who can help them get good jobs. And they can't take time off from any low-paying jobs they do find to look for something better.

Salvadoran workers in these low-paying jobs seem invisible to many people. But these immigrant workers make a huge difference. They do jobs that

WE DON'T EVEN KNOW HOW THEY SURVIVE.

—*Carlos Vaquerano, talking about Salvadorans who work for very low wages because they don't have legal papers* need to be done, but which many other Americans don't want to do. And because workers will take low wages, that keeps costs down. In this way, even Salvadorans who make very little money are making big contributions to America and its economy.

STRESS AND PAINFUL MEMORIES

Many Salvadorans in America still have painful memories of the civil war. People saw family members killed or suffered violence themselves. They often saw fighting and terror near homes, schools, and businesses. The trauma haunts people even many years later.

Moving north breaks apart many families too. Traditionally, the value of *familismo* made family the center of Salvadorans' life and the basic source for their emotional support. When their family units are split apart, many Salvadoran Americans feel that they have lost a major tool for coping with life's challenges. This

I've seen a lot of poverty. . . . But we've always been struggling. I'm sad, but I'm proud at the same time. Every day I come here on the bus and I see all kinds of people struggling, going to work, selling stuff on the street—surviving.

—*Luis Viscarra, a Salvadoran who works with a youth organization in Los Angeles*

loss places further stress on new immigrants.

Family members sometimes come to the United States later, but problems can still arise. Some parents have not seen their children for years, and they might not even recognize each other when they are finally together again. And for children who have missed out on their parents' support and guidance as they grew, rebuilding emotional ties can be very hard.

Even families that stay together face problems. Back in El Salvador, men usually worked outside the home, while women cared for their children and kept house. But in the United States, both partners often need jobs outside the home to make enough money. Men might feel guilty about not being able to provide for their families alone. At the same time, partners have to learn how to share duties at home. Such changes can cause family problems and unhappiness.

Salvadoran children also lead very different lives in the United States than they did in their homeland. Children in El Salvador are expected to be very obedient. But American children are often more independent and outspoken. As Salvadoran children adopt these ways, their parents may have trouble dealing with such different standards. In turn, unruly children may resent adults trying to discipline them. If parents do not have the right legal papers, their children might even threaten to tell the government. Similarly, when they disobey, some children hear threats of being "sent back." Usually, neither the parents nor the children carry out their threats. But the tension adds to stress in the family.

Many Salvadoran families in America also face problems when some members have different legal rights than others. For example, parents may have papers to stay in the United States, at least temporarily, while their children may not. Then parents worry about what might happen if their children can't stay. On the other hand, children born in the United States are automatically American citizens, but their Salvadoran–born parents, brothers, or sisters are not.

Poverty, the language barrier, and other issues add more stress. For Salvadoran families, making a new home in America is not just about finding a place to live. It's about learning to deal with a new culture too.

THE PROBLEM OF GANGS

One of the biggest challenges many young Salvadoran Americans face is pressure to join a gang. These crime-centered groups of teens and young adults have long been a problem in many U.S. cities. But to some Salvadoran youths—especially if they're left alone while parents work at one or more jobs—gangs can seem like a place to belong. Also, children of immigrants may feel torn between their parents' culture and mainstream American culture. To them, gangs are a way to rebel against both cultures.

But gangs are very dangerous. Gangs sometimes rob, beat, or kill people to get money. Gang wars, violence, and drug and alcohol use take lives and ruin health. Many gang members don't live past the age of twenty-five. Members also risk winding up in jail for years. And if they are not citizens, the government can deport them. They may then join gangs in El Salvador and add to crime there.

In 1996 former gang members who had been sent back to El Salvador formed an organization called Homies Unidos (United Homies, or Friends) in San Salvador. Hoping to help other young people stay away from gangs, they started programs in El Salvador. But young Salvadorans in the United States still joined gangs. In 1997 Homies Unidos expanded its work to Los Angeles, where the group's youth programs teach leadership skills, build self-esteem, and promote a healthy lifestyle. Programs in Washington, D.C., San Francisco, and other cities also work to fight the gang problem. As Luis Viscarra at Homies Unidos stresses, "Children have the power to change the future."

HELPING BACK HOME

Even as they make new lives in the United States, Salvadorans rarely forget the people they left behind. Most people still have relatives back home and send money whenever they can.

Salvadoran Americans also support charitable and civic projects in their homeland. After major earthquakes in 2001, for example, Salvadorans in the United States sent money for relief efforts. Money also flowed to El Salvador after the devastation caused by Hurricane Mitch in 1998.

Other aid helps specific towns. Salvadoran soccer star Mauricio Cienfuegos has led efforts to build a major sports complex in La Union. Another group

A Salvadoran woman receives a food handout after the 2001 earthquakes in El Salvador.

I STILL HAVE FAMILY BACK IN EL SALVADOR. WE OBVIOUSLY HELP THEM OUT.

—Arturo Alvarez, Major League Soccer player whose parents fled El Salvador's civil war and settled in Houston, Texas

called SHARE Foundation matches Salvadoran American groups with towns in El Salvador that need help.

Money sent from people in the United States comes to a total of about $2 billion a year, making up El Salvador's top source of income. This money is so important to the country that El Salvador made the U.S. dollar its legal form of money in 2001. But sending money home can also be a huge sacrifice for the many Salvadorans in America who may be working in low-paying jobs and struggling to make ends meet.

A lot of it for me is a way to give back to my people. . . . I feel almost an obligation to help them and return favors to the people of El Salvador.

—Mauricio Cienfuegos, Los Angeles Galaxy coach and player who has raised money for charitable and civic projects in El Salvador

LEGAL ISSUES

Many Salvadorans have a permanent right to live in the United States. But many still don't know for sure whether they will be able to stay.

Some Salvadorans have become citizens of the United States. Citizens have many rights. They can vote, run in political races, and travel freely in the country. They also have duties, such as serving on juries.

Salvadorans can also become permanent residents. Every permanent resident has a legal paper called a green card—even though it is not green—that lets the resident stay in the United States as long as he or she wants. Still other Salvadorans have papers called visas, which allow them to stay for a shorter time. A visa may let a person hold a job or go to school.

For Salvadorans who came into the country illegally, things are more complicated. Over the years, Salvadorans have fought legal battles to be able to stay in the United States. They filed a lawsuit so that the government would consider their asylum requests.

Many Salvadorans still come to America in hopes of providing their children with better lives than they had in El Salvador.

They worked to get helpful laws passed and are still working to improve immigration laws.

Thanks to that work, many Salvadorans in America got a right to new hearings. Many others got temporary permission to stay in the United States. As a result, they have been able to build safer, better lives for themselves and their families. However, thousands of people do not know if they can stay in the United States permanently. Often they have lived in the United States for a long time. They worry that if they eventually must go back to El Salvador, their hard work here will have been for nothing.

Still other people may have no legal right to stay in the United States. If government officials find them, they can be sent back to El Salvador right away. For these people, life is most uncertain of all.

AS ALL OF THESE SALVADORANS HAVE COME UP HERE, ONE OF THE DRIVING FACTORS IS TO HAVE OPPORTUNITY FOR THEIR CHILDREN, TO FIND A BETTER WORLD.

—Ana Sol Gutiérrez, Salvadoran American state politician in Maryland

BUILDING STRONGER COMMUNITIES

Salvadoran Americans have formed strong communities in the United States. Many Salvadorans have started new businesses to help their people. Import companies bring in cheeses and other foods from El Salvador. Local Hispanic groceries sell those foods. Some businesses help send money and other gifts back to El Salvador, and a Salvadoran bank has opened a branch in Los Angeles.

Meanwhile, more Americans are learning about Salvadoran culture. Salvadoran Americans live in more than 150 U.S. cities, from Phoenix, Arizona, to Minneapolis, Minnesota. Many cities now have Salvadoran restaurants. Salvadoran American dancers perform in Washington, D.C., and other cities. Many museums display Salvadoran art.

Salvadoran restaurants are becoming a common site in many U.S. cities, such as this one in New York City. Find links for more information about the many ways that people of Salvadoran heritage contribute to life in America at www.inamericabooks.com.

PUPUSAS AND CURTIDO

Pupusas are a unique Salvadoran food. These stuffed corn tortillas have a filling of cheese, refried beans, or cooked shredded meat. Salvadorans and Salvadoran Americans enjoy them with tomato salsa and a vinegar-based coleslaw called *curtido*. Try this simplified recipe. And remember to be careful with all kitchen appliances. Ask an adult if you need help. To learn how to prepare other Salvadoran dishes, visit www.inamericabooks.com.

CURTIDO:

2 C. SHREDDED GREEN CABBAGE

1 LARGE CARROT, PEELED AND
     GRATED

1 TBSP. CANNED CHOPPED GREEN
     CHILI PEPPERS

4 TBSP. WHITE VINEGAR

$^1/_4$ TSP. SALT

$^1/_4$ TSP. SUGAR

$^1/_4$ TSP. GROUND BLACK PEPPER

CHEESE PUPUSAS:

$3^1/_4$ C. MASA HARINA (CORN
     FLOUR SOLD AT ETHNIC
     GROCERIES)

1 TSP. SALT

$1^1/_2$ C. WATER

2 C. SHREDDED MONTEREY JACK
     CHEESE

3 TBSP. VEGETABLE OIL

$^1/_2$ C. SALSA

1. Mix curtido ingredients in a large bowl. Taste and adjust seasonings, if desired. Cover and refrigerate for an hour.
2. For pupusa dough, combine masa harina, salt, and water in a large bowl. Knead mixture until it feels like playdough. Cover the dough with a light towel and let it sit for about 10 minutes. Meanwhile, set out 12 to 16 pieces of waxed paper, about 8 x 11 inches each.

3. Shape dough into portions the size and shape of an egg. Holding a dough "egg" in one hand, press the dough with your other hand's thumb in to make an indentation. Keep pressing until the dough resembles a small deep cup with thin sides. Pack cheese into the dough, and squish the top edges together. With your hands, gently roll the stuffed dough into a ball.

4. Put the ball about 3 inches in from the short edge of a piece of waxed paper. Fold waxed paper over the ball. Gently press your hand on top of the waxed paper to flatten the ball until it measures about 4 inches across and between $1/4$- and $1/2$-inch thick. Smooth the outer edge by running your fingertips over the waxed paper and around the pupusa.

5. Repeat steps 3 and 4 with the remaining dough.

6. Heat 1 tablespoon of the vegetable oil in a skillet or flat griddle on medium heat. Peel the top layer of waxed paper off a pupusa. Then flip the pupusa onto a large flat spatula and peel the paper off. Plop the pupusa onto the skillet.

7. Cook pupusas about two minutes on each side, until golden brown. Repeat with the remaining pupusas, adding oil as needed.

8. Serve pupusas with salsa and curtido on the side.

Serves 6

While Salvadorans remain a small part of the total U.S. population, they have strong community organizations. In the Los Angeles area, the Salvadoran American Leadership and Educational Fund, or SALEF, gives out scholarships. The group also urges Salvadoran American citizens to vote and gets people involved in politics. CARECEN, the Central American Resource Center in Los Angeles, has offices in several cities. The group offers counseling and helps people find jobs.

Still other groups are just for fun. Social clubs and church groups give people a place to get together. Soccer clubs are popular too.

FIND LINKS FOR MORE INFORMATION ABOUT SALVADORAN ORGANIZATIONS AND CLUBS IN AMERICA AT WWW.INAMERICABOOKS.COM.

The Salvadorans who come to the United States are creating new lives while still celebrating their strong heritage.

Like many other groups, Salvadorans came to the United States for a better life. They wanted to escape an awful war. They wanted their children to have more opportunities. Over the years, Salvadoran Americans have achieved many of these goals. And they have also become an important part of American culture.

They still face many challenges, but they face them with hope.

"The United States still is keeping the tradition of being a welcoming land," adds Saul Solorzano at CARECEN–DC. "People that face persecution, as the Pilgrims did, can still find a place in this country to make a life without fear."

FAMOUS SALVADORAN AMERICANS

ARTURO ALVAREZ (b. 1985)

"My first present as a little boy was a soccer ball," says Arturo Alvarez. His parents fled El Salvador's civil war in the early 1980s. Alvarez was born in Houston and grew up to become a professional soccer player. "Soccer is pretty big in the Latin countries," notes Alvarez. "I grew up loving it. It's my dream." The San Jose Earthquakes picked Alvarez in the 2003 Major League Soccer SuperDraft. "Scoring my first major league soccer goal stands out a lot," says Alvarez. That late-in-the-game goal on June 14, 2003, gave the Earthquakes a 2–1 victory over the Dallas Burn. Alvarez has also played on national youth teams and competed internationally for the United States. Alvarez's sports career is on the rise, but he remains very concerned about El Salvador and its people. "I am proud to have Salvadoran blood in me," says Alvarez. "That is something that I'm always going to keep in mind."

JORGE ARGUETA (b. 1961)

Poet and author Jorge Argueta was born in San Salvador. As a boy, he loved riding horses and playing in the rivers of rural El Salvador. He learned about his Indian heritage from his grandmother, a traditional Indian healer.

Jorge also enjoyed listening to all the stories people told at the small restaurant his family owned in San Salvador. But in 1980, El Salvador's civil war forced Jorge to flee to San Francisco. "In my heart, I carried a lot of sadness, because I had left behind the people that I loved," says Jorge. Working in a coffeehouse, Jorge learned English. Soon he began writing poems about the anguish and loneliness of the war. Over time, however, Jorge felt himself grow bitter and angry until, he said, "I only saw darkness." Then a friend invited him to a Native American ceremony. Staring into the fire, Jorge remembered his grandmother and all the beauty he once loved. "It reminded me of that child that was still inside of me and wanted to be happy and wanted to have a change in life," says Jorge. "So I had some hope again." That hope and Jorge's love of beauty show in his various books for children, including *A Movie in My Pillow* and *Xochitl and the Flowers*. He continues to write books for children and has more due out soon.

MARIO BENCASTRO (b. 1949)

Author and playwright Mario Bencastro was born in Ahuachapán, El Salvador. He left El Salvador

during the civil war and joined the Salvadoran community in Washington, D.C. "Like thousands of Salvadorans, I came to the U.S. to look for a better life for my family, and opportunities to develop my craft," Bencastro says. He sees himself as a historian of the conflicts and hopes of his people. Bencastro writes a lot of fiction. Yet his characters' conflicts come from real life. Some of Bencastro's stories and poems talk about the civil war.

Other stories tell about immigrants' struggles. Bencastro has also written a young adult book called *Voyage to the Land of Grandfather*. It deals with issues Salvadoran youths face in America. He often talks at schools and with youth groups. He wants people to know about El Salvador's history and its people's problems. Bencastro started out as a painter back in El Salvador. He has also worked as a computer analyst. But he loves writing the most. That lets him tell people about Salvadorans' struggles.

ROSIE CASALS (b. 1948)

Rosie Casals started playing tennis at aged eight. She often played at Golden Gate Park in San Francisco. That's her hometown. Casals's great-uncle and adoptive father, Manuel Casals y Bordas, was her first coach. Like Casals's birth parents, he came to the United States from El Salvador. Casals became a champion tennis player. At just over five feet two inches tall, Casals was shorter than many

players. She made up for it with speed and energy. She played an aggressive game. During the 1960s, many tennis players were rich. They trained with pros at country clubs. Casals practiced on public tennis courts. The family scrimped to save the money that Casals needed to enter tournaments. For eleven years, Casals was one of America's top five women tennis players. She won many big competitions. In 1973 Casals won the first Family Circle Cup. At the time, the thirty-thousand-dollar prize was the highest award ever for any female athlete. Casals worked hard to make tennis a professional sport. She also fought to get equality in pay, prize money, and playing conditions for women tennis players. She was inducted into the International Tennis Hall of Fame in 1996. Casals still plays in tennis events. She has written articles and done television commentary, and also started her own company, Sportswoman, Inc. The company sets up and promotes tennis events.

MAURICIO CIENFUEGOS

(b. 1968) Mauricio Cienfuegos grew up playing soccer in San Salvador. In 1985 he began his professional soccer career. He joined El Salvador's National Team in 1987. He has

played in more than seventy-five international matches. Cienfuegos joined the Los Angeles Galaxy in 1996. It was the team's first season. Through 2003 he played in more than two hundred Major League Soccer games. In 2003 he announced that he would move into coaching. "When I first came here I didn't realize how many Salvadorans were in Los Angeles, and didn't realize it was going to be as emotional an experience as it's been," says Cienfuegos. Over the years, the Salvadoran community has cheered him on. In many ways, Cienfuegos feels like he's carried a torch for his people. Cienfuegos has worked with many community groups. He has been very active in raising money to help people back home in El Salvador. "Whether there are earthquakes or not in El Salvador, there are still needy people there, and people that need our help," he says. Cienfuegos lives with his wife and their children in the United States, but the family visits El Salvador too. In his view, "it's very important to tell children where you came from, where you were born, where you were raised, where your roots are."

LIZ FIGUEROA (b. 1951)

Liz Figueroa was born in San Francisco. Both her parents came from El Salvador. As a state politician, Figueroa has helped many people—both Salvadorans and other Americans. Before holding public office, Figueroa owned Figueroa Employment Consultants. Her company helped injured workers get new jobs. Figueroa has also served on the board of directors of the Union Sanitary District. She was the district's first female president. Figueroa began serving in the California state legislature in 1995. After serving in the assembly for two terms, she was elected to the state senate. Figueroa has worked hard on many causes. She works to improve health care, simplify laws that affect businesses, and protect consumers. Figueroa cares very deeply about woman's rights and also speaks out on human rights issues. Several organizations have named Figueroa as Legislator of the Year. They include the March of Dimes, the American Academy of Pediatrics, and other groups.

LILO GONZALEZ (b. 1957)

Born in Armenia, El Salvador, Lilo Gonzalez was a schoolteacher in his home country. But when he came to the United States in 1981 and settled in the Washington, D.C., area, he had to work as a dishwasher to support his family. During this lonely time, Lilo taught himself to play the guitar and began singing at a

coffeehouse. Many of his songs explore the plight of new immigrants. Others deal with social problems, such as community violence. Lilo has won various awards for his music and has toured the United States with his band. Lilo has also taught music to young people and been active in groups promoting the arts in Washington's Latino community. But Lilo has not forgotten his hometown of Armenia, either. After witnessing the 2001 earthquake there, Lilo raised money for relief efforts and continues to support projects in the town.

ANA SOL GUTIÉRREZ (b. 1942)

Ana Sol Gutiérrez has served the

public as an elected official in Maryland. She is also an aeronautical engineer. Gutiérrez was born in Santa Ana, El Salvador, but her family moved to Maryland when she was little. "My father was one of the original founding directors of the World Bank and the IMF [International Monetary Fund]," explains Gutiérrez. After attending college and graduate school, Gutiérrez worked as a college professor and an aeronautical engineer in Bolivia, Peru, and Venezuela. She moved back to the United States and continued her work in the aerospace field. In 1990 Gutiérrez was elected to the Montgomery County Board of Education in Maryland. She became the first person of Salvadoran descent elected to public office in the United States. Gutiérrez's election followed a long history of her involvement in civic affairs, including work with the Montgomery County Parent-Teacher Association, the National Council of La Raza, the League of United Latin American Citizens, and other groups. In 2002 Gutiérrez ran for the Maryland House of Delegates and won the election. She began serving her term in 2003.

KARLISIMA (b. 1970) Born in San
Salvador as Karla Cecilia Rodas Cortez, Karlisima is an award–winning artist. She began formal art classes at the age of seven and kept pursuing her passion for art after coming to the Washington, D.C., area in 1984 at the age of 14. Karlisima's talent won her a

scholarship to Washington University in Saint Louis, Missouri, where she majored in painting. Karlisima's work has been displayed in various cities across the United States, as well as in Europe and El Salvador. Many of Karlisima's paintings and murals suggest an imaginary or mythical world. Her work also explores themes of meditation, prayer, and worship. The bold, bright colors reflect the natural beauty of Karlisima's native El Salvador, as well as her Mayan ancestry.

RUBÉN MARTÍNEZ (b. 1962)

Rubén Martínez was born in Los Angeles to a Salvadoran mother and a Mexican father. Martínez draws on his Hispanic roots in his work as a journalist, book author, and poet. Martínez's writing often reflects the concerns and experiences of Hispanics. His book *Crossing Over* is about a Mexican migrant family. *The Other Side* is a collection of articles and poems set in Los Angeles, Mexico, and El Salvador. Martínez has been a writer for the *L.A. Weekly*. He has also been an associate editor for *Pacific News Service*. He has been a television news commentator and taught college journalism too.

CHRISTY TURLINGTON

(b. 1969) Model Christy Turlington was born in California. Her father was an American airline pilot. Her mother came from El Salvador. Turlington's face has been seen  around the world in ads for cosmetics and fragrances. She was also used as a model for mannequins at the New York Metropolitan Museum of Art's Costume Institute. She's been on the covers of *Elle*, *Cosmopolitan*, and *Glamour*. Turlington is an outspoken champion of social causes. She's been a spokesperson for antismoking campaigns sponsored by the Centers for Disease Control and Prevention and the American Cancer Society. Turlington also helps people in El Salvador. She donated money from a 1995 photo calendar to the American Foundation for El Salvador. She has also chaired a group to build a library, gallery, and community technology center in San Salvador.

TIMELINE

3000–1500 B.C.	Early civilizations settle in El Salvador.
A.D. 300–1000	El Salvador is part of the Mayan Empire.
1100– early 1500s	The Pipils become the main tribe. Their culture thrives.
1524	Spanish captain Pedro de Alvarado first tries to conquer El Salvador.
1525	The Spanish return and conquer the area.
1821	Spain grants independence to Central America.
1823	El Salvador joins United Provinces of Central America.
1841	El Salvador adopts a constitution and becomes an independent country.
1840s–1850s	El Salvador begins growing coffee.
1860s–1920s	Salvadoran laws gradually take away the land where many peasants grew their own food, allowing wealthy landowners to grow more coffee.
1929	The Great Depression begins.
1932	In La Matanza, or the slaughter, the Salvadoran government kills thirty thousand people after a failed revolt by Communist leader Augustin Farabundo Martí. Pipil culture fades after that.
1969	The "100-hour" Soccer War breaks out between El Salvador and Honduras, sending about 200,000 Salvadorans back to El Salvador.

1970s	Outbreaks of violence grow in El Salvador as the government silences its critics. Rebel groups want to change the social system.
1979	A group of civilians and army leaders takes over the Salvadoran government but cannot stop the army's violence against peasants.
1980	In March the murder of Archbishop Oscar Romero sets off El Salvador's civil war between the army and rebel groups, known as Farabundo Martí National Liberation Front (FMLN).
1980s	Salvadorans flee to the United States to escape the civil war. Despite protests about human rights violations, the United States sends El Salvador's government hundreds of millions of dollars in aid each year. Meanwhile, the U.S. government gets tougher on enforcing laws to keep out undocumented immigrants.
1982	U.S. church groups start the Sanctuary Movement to help refugees from Central America.
1983	Salvadorans in the United States start the group that is now called the Central American Resource Center (CARECEN) in Los Angeles.
1985	*American Baptist Churches v. Thornburgh*, or the ABC case, is filed. The case charges that the U.S. government has unfairly denied asylum to Salvadorans and Guatemalans fleeing from civil war.
1986	The Immigration Reform and Control Act makes it harder for people who come into the United States illegally to get jobs. A major earthquake strikes El Salvador.

1989	Salvadoran rebels begin their "final offensive" in the civil war, and the army strikes back with added violence.
1990	Under the 1990 Immigration Act, Salvadoran immigrants receive Temporary Protected Status (TPS). TPS gives immigrants permission to stay in the United States for a limited time, even if they came in illegally, if sending them away could cause danger or hardship. Ana Sol Gutiérrez becomes the first person of Salvadoran descent elected to public office in the United States.
1992	In January the Salvadoran government and rebel groups sign the Chapultepec Peace Accords. The treaty ends the civil war.
1993	The United Nations' Truth Commission issues its report on El Salvador.
1994	The Contemporary Dance Theater of El Salvador is founded in San Salvador and begins performing in the Washington, D.C., area.
1995	Community leaders in Los Angeles start SALEF, the Salvadoran American Leadership and Educational Fund.
1996	Changes to immigration and welfare laws make life harder for immigrants in the United States. Rosie Casals enters the International Tennis Hall of Fame.
1998	Hurricane Mitch ravages Central America. In the United States, Liz Figueroa is elected to the California State Senate.

2001   A major earthquake hits El Salvador, and the United States again gives Temporary Protected Status to Salvadorans. It later extends TPS several times.

2004   A federal court in California finds former Salvadoran military commander Alvaro Rafael Saravia took part in the assassination of Archbishop Oscar Romero and holds the murder was a "crime against humanity."

2005   U.S. Citizenship and Immigration Services again extends TPS for about 248,000 Salvadorans in the United States.

GLOSSARY

ASYLUM: legal protection for people who are afraid, unwilling, or unable to go back to their country because of persecution

BARRIO: a neighborhood where Spanish is spoken and most residents are Hispanic

CITIZEN: someone who belongs to a country. Citizens have special rights that the government gives members of its country, but they also have responsibilities.

CIVIL WAR: a war between people living in the same country

COMMUNISM: a type of political and economic system. In a Communist country, the government controls ownership of goods and services.

COYOTE: a person who agrees, for a price, to smuggle immigrants into the United States illegally

DEPORT: to send someone away from a country and forbid that person to return

EMIGRATE: to leave one's home country to live somewhere else. A person who emigrates is called an emigrant.

HISPANIC: a person living in the United States who is of Central American, South American, or Mexican heritage. "Latino" means basically the same thing.

IMMIGRATE: to come to live in a country other than one's homeland. A person who immigrates is called an immigrant.

MIGRATION CHAIN: a pattern of immigrants moving to places where other people from their country went before them

MISSIONARY: a person who works for a church or religious group and who usually tries to convert other people to that religion. Spanish missionaries in El Salvador worked to convert the Pipils to Catholicism.

PEASANTS: rural people, often uneducated, who traditionally supported themselves by growing their own food on small plots of land

THINGS TO SEE AND DO

CELEBRATE HISPANIC HERITAGE
MONTH
http://www.historychannel.com/
classroom/hhm
http://www.galegroup.com/
free_resources/chh
Cities across the United States hold festivals and special events for Hispanic Heritage Month, beginning September 15. The date marks Independence Day for El Salvador, as well as four other Latin American countries. Attend a concert, parade, or art display. Or check out special displays at your local library or community center.

SAMPLE SALVADORAN FOOD
http://www.settlement.org/cp/
english/elsalvador/eating.html
The Washington, D.C., area has about 150 Salvadoran restaurants, ranging from snack bars to fancy sit-down places. Many other U.S. cities offer Salvadoran food too. Immigrant families often run the restaurants and make favorite foods from home.

SEE THE CONTEMPORARY DANCE
THEATER OF EL SALVADOR
http://www.elsalvador.org/home.nsf/
culture
This professional dance company performs classic and modern dance at various places around the Washington, D.C., area from April to October. You might also see Salvadoran folk dances at Hispanic festivals around the United States.

VISIT A GALLERY OR MUSEUM
Several galleries in the United States feature Salvadoran artists. The museums include the Museum of Latin American Art in Long Beach, California (at http://www .molaa.com), the Consulate of El Salvador Art Gallery in Washington, D.C., and the Oakland Museum of California (at http://www.museumca .org).

VISIT A LOCAL FESTIVAL
http://www.elsalvador.org/home.nsf/
community
The Salvadoran Embassy's website lists events for Salvadorans in cities across the United States. August and September are especially busy months.

SOURCE NOTES

11 Karen Hong, "The Land of the Jewel," *Faces*, November 1998, 27–28.

12 Steffen W. Schmidt, *El Salvador: America's Next Vietnam?* (Salisbury, NC: Documentary Publications, 1983), 35.

13 El Comité Pro-Centenario José Matías Delgado, *José Matías Delgado, Padre de la Patria* (San Salvador: Ministerio de Educacion Departamento Editorial, 1932), 135.

15 Alberto Masferrer, "La Crisis del Maíz [The Corn Crisis]," *Patria*, January 18, 1929, quoted in *Latin American Politics and Development*, ed. Howard J. Wiarda and Harvey F. Kline (Boulder, CO: Westview Press, 2000), 476.

16 Thomas P. Anderson, *Matanza*, 2nd. ed. (Wilimantic, CT: Curbstone Press, 1992), 173.

25 Carlos Vaquerano, SALEF, telephone interview with author, November 21, 2003.

26 The Commission on the Truth for El Salvador, "From Madness to Hope: The 12-Year War in El Salvador," March 15, 1993, http://www.usip.org/library/tc/doc/reports/el_salvador/tc_es_03151993_toc.html (February 10, 2005).

29 Saul Solorzano, executive director, CARECEN–DC, telephone interview with author, November 24, 2003.

36 Patrick Young, CARECEN–NY, telephone interview with author, September 4, 2003.

42 Commission on the Truth for El Salvador, "From Madness to Hope," 115.

42 *Doe v. Saravia*, U.S. District Court, E.D. California, Case No. Civ-F-03-6249, Findings of Fact and Conclusions of Law, November 23, 2004, 87.

43 Dina López, Ohio State University, telephone interview with author, September 17, 2003.

45 Patrick Young, telephone interview.

48 Carlos Vaquerano, telephone interview.

49 Luis Viscarra, Homies Unidos, Los Angeles, telephone interview with author, September 8, 2003.

51 Ibid.

52 Arturo Alvarez, San Jose Earthquakes, telephone interview with author, September 10, 2003.

53 Mauricio Cienfuegos, Los Angeles Galaxy, telephone interview with author, September 26, 2003.

54 Ana Sol Gutiérrez, Maryland House of Delegates, telephone interview with author, October 6, 2003.

59 Saul Solorzano, telephone interview.

60 Arturo Alvarez, telephone interview.

60–61 Jorge Argueta, telephone interview with author, January 31, 2005.

61 Mario Bencastro, e-mail communication to author, September 28, 2003.

62–63 Mauricio Cienfuegos, telephone interview.

64 Ana Sol Gutiérrez, telephone interview.

69 *Doe v. Saravia*, 87.

SELECTED BIBLIOGRAPHY

Baker–Cristales, Beth. *Salvadoran Migration to Southern California: Redefining El Hermano Lejano.* Gainesville: University Press of Florida, 2004. This book focuses on how Salvadoran immigrants around Los Angeles have maintained strong ties to their homeland.

Coutin, Susan Bibler. *Legalizing Moves: Salvadoran Immigrants' Struggle for U.S. Residency.* Ann Arbor: University of Michigan Press, 2000. This book details approaches Salvadorans have tried so they could stay in the United States legally: going to court; using and seeking changes to the law; working with agencies; and swaying public opinion.

Hamilton, Nora, and Norma Stoltz Chinchilla. *Seeking Community in a Global City: Guatemalans and Salvadorans in Los Angeles.* Philadelphia: Temple University Press, 2001. This book explores how large numbers of people from El Salvador and Guatemala came to live in the Los Angeles area and explores the challenges facing them as they build new lives.

Mahler, Sarah J. *American Dreaming: Immigrant Life on the Margins.* Princeton, NJ: Princeton University Press, 1995. This book examines how and why people went to Long Island from El Salvador, along with the problems that the new arrivals faced.

——. *Salvadorans in Suburbia: Symbiosis and Conflict.* Boston: Allyn & Bacon, 1995. This book tells about the everyday struggles of Salvadorans on Long Island. It also looks at conflicts they face among themselves and with other groups.

Marsiglia, Flavio Francisco, and Cecilia Menjívar. "Nicaraguan and Salvadoran Children and Families." In *Culturally Competent Practice with Immigrant and Refugee Children and Families,* edited by Rowena Fong. New York: Guilford Press, 2004. This article explores social problems faced by Salvadorans in the United States and explores their cultural values.

Menjívar, Cecilia. *Fragmented Ties: Salvadoran Immigrant Networks in America.* Berkeley: University of California Press, 2000. Salvadorans came to the United States for a safer and better life, but often they faced poverty, legal difficulties, and other problems. This book looks at Salvadorans' experiences in this country.

"The Odyssey of Salvadoran Asylum Seekers." *NACLA Report on the Americas,* May/June 2004, 38. This article sums up how Salvadorans have tried to stay in the United States and updates the debate on immigration reform to 2004.

Orellana, Marjorie, et al. "Transnational Childhoods: The Participation of Children in Processes of Family Migration." *Social Problems,* November 2001, 573–592. This study looks at how migration affects children and their families, focusing on Salvadorans and other groups.

Popkin, Eric. "Transnational Migration and Development in Postwar Peripheral States: An Examination of Guatemalan and

Salvadoran State Linkages with Their Migrant Populations in Los Angeles." *Current Sociology*, May/July 2003, 347–374. Popkin's article tells how Central American immigrants in Los Angeles help people back home, with encouragement from El Salvador's current government.

Repak, Terry A. *Waiting on Washington: Central American Workers in the Nation's Capital.* Philadelphia: Temple University Press, 1995. This book shows how Salvadoran and other Central American workers came to Washington, D.C., as domestic workers in the 1960s and 1970s and later brought friends and family to the city during El Salvador's civil war.

Vigil, James Diego. *A Rainbow of Gangs: Street Cultures in the Mega-City.* Austin: University of Texas Press, 2002. Chapter nine of this book describes street culture among Salvadoran youth in Los Angeles's Pico-Union area.

FURTHER READING & WEBSITES

NONFICTION

Bachelis, Faren. *The Central Americans.* New York: Chelsea House Publishers, 1990. This book looks at culture, history, and religion in Central America and explores factors that led people to emigrate from there to North America.

Behnke, Alison, in consultation with Griselda Aracely Chacon and Kristina Anderson. *Cooking the Central American Way.* Minneapolis: Lerner Publications Company, 2005. This cultural cookbook presents recipes for authentic and traditional Central American dishes, including Salvadoran pupusas and horchata (rice milk).

Cheney, Glenn Alan. *El Salvador, Country in Crisis.* New York: Franklin Watts, 1990. This book examines how El Salvador's civil war drove huge numbers of Salvadorans to come to the United States.

Deem, James M. *El Salvador.* Berkeley Heights, NJ: MyReportLinks.com Books, 2004. This book describes El Salvador and describes how people came from there to the United States.

"El Salvador." *Faces*, November 1998. This issue of *Faces* magazine showcases El Salvador's history and culture.

Morrison, Marion. *El Salvador.* New York: Children's Press, 2001. This book explores El Salvador and issues facing the country.

Sanders, Renfield. *El Salvador.* Philadelphia: Chelsea House, 1999. This book gives a detailed account of El Salvador's history and its culture.

Schwabach, Karen. *El Salvador: On the Road to Peace.* Parsippany, NJ: Dillon Press, 1999. This book looks at El Salvador's challenges after the civil war.

Shields, Charles J. *El Salvador.* Philadelphia: Mason Crest Publishers, 2003. This book describes El Salvador's culture and the challenges facing the country today. It includes information about festivals and recipes too.

FICTION

Argueta, Jorge. *A Movie in My Pillow: Poems.* San Francisco: Children's Book Press, 2001. Poems and pictures show what it was like for a Salvadoran boy to move to San Francisco's Mission District with his father. The text has both English and Spanish versions.

Bencastro, Mario. *Viaje a la Tierra del Abuelo.* Houston: Arte Publico Press, 2004. This book's title in English means "Voyage to the Land of Grandfather," and it's written for children who can read Spanish. The story tells about a Los Angeles teen's trip back to El Salvador.

Buss, Fran Leeper, with Daisy Cubias. *Journey of the Sparrows.* 1991. Reprint, New York: Puffin Books, 2002. This book tells the story of Maria and her family as they move from El Salvador to the United States.

Covington, Dennis. *Lasso the Moon.* New York: Delacorte Press, 1995. A teenage girl becomes friends with a Salvadoran refugee who is in the United States illegally.

Howlett, Bud. *I'm New Here.* Boston: Houghton Mifflin Company, 1993. Jazmin conquers challenges at her new school in the United States.

Lainez, René Colato. *Waiting for Papá.* Houston: Arte Publico Press, 2004. With text in both English and Spanish, this story tells about Beto's new life in the United States with his mother. He can hardly wait for his father to join them from El Salvador.

Temple, Frances. *Grab Hands and Run.* New York: Orchard Books, 1993. After his father disappears, a twelve-year-old boy flees from El Salvador with his mother and sister.

WEBSITES

CENTRAL AMERICAN RESOURCE CENTER (CARECEN)
http://www.carecensf.org/
http://www.carecen-la.org/index2.html
http://www.icomm.ca/carecen/index.html
http://www.dccarecen.org/
CARECEN's different offices provide a range of services to immigrants from Central America.

EMBASSY OF EL SALVADOR
http://www.elsalvador.org/home.nsf/home
The Salvadoran Embassy's website gives information about El Salvador,

Salvadorans' activities in the United States, cultural events, and more.

INAMERICABOOKS.COM
http://www.inamericabooks.com
Visit inamericabooks.com, the online home of the In America series, to get linked to all sorts of useful information. You'll find historical and cultural websites related to individual groups, as well as general information on genealogy, creating your own family tree, and the history of immigration in America.

SALVADORAN AMERICAN LEADERSHIP AND EDUCATIONAL FUND (SALEF)
http://www.salef.org
SALEF's goal is to promote civic participation and representation of Salvadorans in U.S. society.

U.S. CITIZENSHIP AND IMMIGRATION SERVICES
http://uscis.gov/graphics/index.htm
This federal agency deals with immigrants and the circumstances under which they can live in the United States and become citizens.

INDEX

web enhanced at **www.inamericabooks.com**

AUTHOR ACKNOWLEDGMENTS

The author gratefully thanks the following people for sharing their insights and offering other help with this book: Arturo Alvarez, San Jose Earthquakes; Nick Ammazzalorso and Patrick Donnelly, Los Angeles Galaxy; Jorge Argueta; Mario Bencastro; Simon Borg, Major League Soccer; Maria Burguera; Mauricio Cienfuegos, Los Angeles Galaxy; Lilio Gonzalez; Ana Sol Gutiérrez, Maryland legislature; Dina López, Ohio University; Laura Meissner; Cecilia Menjívar, Arizona State University; Jed Mettee, San Jose Earthquakes; Nestor Rodriguez, University of Houston; Rose Robinson, University of California Press; Saul Solorzano, executive director, CARECEN-DC; Carlos Antonio H. Vaquerano, executive director, SALEF; Luis Viscarra, Homies Unidos, Los Angeles; Patrick Young, CARECEN-N.Y.